Hannah Widell & Amanda Schulman

Photos Amelia Widell

SWEDISH SUMMER FEASTS

Favorite Recipes for Picnics, Brunches, and Barbecues by the Beach

Translated by
Paulina Björk Kapsalis

Skyhorse Publishing

Contents

Welcome

Welcome to our world and our magical summers!

Summer is magical. It's not just the sunshine that we love, but also the fact that summers in Sweden are when we create our strongest memories. It's when we have time for each other, time to spend together and cook food. We can finally gather in our country home after having been far apart all winter.

A large portion of our time in the country is spent cooking tons of food. We love food and the whole social aspect that comes with it. Every situation can be enriched with good food—a birthday, a rainy day, a moment with your best friend in the sun on the front steps, a midsummer celebration, or just enjoying the peace and quiet for a while in front of the sauna. That's why we turn every meal, large or small, into a feast.

We are not chefs, and we never cook things we can't manage. We believe that knowing how to cook is useful to everyone. We're no snobs, and we don't pretend to be something that we're not—we cook like normal people do and hope to inspire with our lust for the good, the tasty, and the beautiful. We often say that we like to laugh until we cry and cry until we laugh again. This book is inspired by that. This book holds all kinds of feelings, and we like to share them, along with our best recipes and cooking advice.

We want to share our magical summers with the world, because they are our absolute favorite thing. It's going to be wonderful!

All Kärlek
Nadine Amanda ♡

The First Day of Summer

I think this may be the best day of the whole year. We are on our way to our little home in the country, climbing up the gravel path leading up to the house. The ditch is lined with flowers, and we marvel at the sight of the little lambs in the meadow next to our yard. They watch us too as we pass. We reach the barn, walk through the knee-high grass. Swallows flit through the air. There is something about the light in June. It's sometimes blinding. The air is clear and it's almost too cold to call this summer, but it doesn't matter. Our whole bodies tingle with the joy of knowing that an entire summer lies ahead of us.

You can feel safe here. I've felt it so many times before. I remember when I was a kid and something was troubling me. It could have been a mean girl at school, or a boy who didn't notice me. These problems would consume all of my thoughts. Unhappy, or with a broken heart, I packed my bags and left for the country house with my family. As soon as we left the city and came here, to the most beautiful place on Earth, all my troubles seemed to disappear. It is still like that today, even though the problems are bigger and more grown up.

There is so much anticipation and joy on that first evening in the country. What is this summer going to be like? Then and there, I feel like the best summer of my life lies before me. Whether that's true or not, it really doesn't matter on that first evening. Eat all of the summer's flavors at once, look up at the sky that is yours, take a sip of a cold drink, and savor that moment. It's alright if this is as good as it gets, because this is perfection.

—Amanda

Strawberries with Prosciutto

Hull the strawberries and wrap each one in half a slice of prosciutto. Place them on a pretty serving plate, drizzle with some olive oil, and top with freshly ground black pepper.

4–6 SERVINGS
½ cup (500 g) fresh strawberries
3 ½ oz (100 g) prosciutto
olive oil
black pepper

Entrecôte with Herb Butter & Grilled Vegetables

Use whatever herbs you have on hand for the herb butter. If you have early spring vegetables, you can grill them whole. If not, split them in half. The potatoes should be split in half either way. For more evenly cooked-through potatoes, blanch them for 5–10 minutes before grilling.

Herb butter: Let the butter soften a bit at room temperature.

Mince the garlic and chop the rosemary. Use a fork to mix the herbs and garlic with the butter. Shape the butter into a log and cover it with plastic wrap. Place it in the freezer until firm.

Place the butter on a plate and slice it. Sprinkle a generous amount of pink peppercorns and sea salt on top.

Grilled vegetables: Brush the potatoes and the rest of the vegetables with olive oil. Add salt and pepper to taste. Grill until browned and tender (use a fork to be sure).

Grill the entrecôte. Season with salt and pepper.

Serve immediately so that the herb butter melts on the hot meat and vegetables.

1 5–7 oz (150–200 g) slice of
    entrecôte steak per person

HERB BUTTER:
7 oz (200 g) butter
3 garlic cloves
1 small bunch of fresh rosemary
whole pink peppercorns
sea salt

GRILLED VEGETABLES:
carrots
asparagus
onion
new potatoes
olive oil
salt and pepper

Summer Gino with Rhubarbs

Peel your rhubarb stalks if they are thick, and chop them into ½ inch (1 cm) pieces. Divide the rhubarb over six pieces of aluminum foil, and top with chocolate pieces the same size as the rhubarb. There should be almost as much chocolate as there is rhubarb. Fold the aluminum foil to make little packages, and grill for about 10 minutes. Serve with ice cream and garnish with sprigs of mint.

6 SERVINGS
3–4 rhubarb stalks
14 oz (400 g) white chocolate

TO SERVE:
vanilla ice cream
sprigs of fresh mint

Midsummer

Swedish summer comes hand in hand with midsummer, an annual Swedish summer holiday that goes on for five weeks. Midsummer Eve has been celebrated for ages, and it is one of our biggest traditions. We dance around the maypole, eat pickled herring, and drink snaps. Midsummer Eve is the ultimate romanticized summer dream. We celebrate the start of summer, and right then and there, nature is at its most beautiful. The flowers are perfect, the air is fragrant, and the sun never sets.

So every year we throw a party. We cook exquisite food, and children and adults celebrate together into the night.

—Hannah

Pickled Herring Dip

Chop the pickled herring. Peel and chop the eggs into small pieces. Finely chop the onion. Mix all the ingredients in a bowl. Season to taste with pepper, and add salt if you want to. To serve, add a dollop of pickled herring dip to a piece of hard rye bread, and garnish with whitefish roe or caviar, dill, and chives.

4 ½ oz (125 g) pickled herring
4 hard-boiled eggs
1 red onion
3 ⅓ tbsp (50 ml) crème fraîche
3 tbsp chopped dill
3 tbsp chopped chives
white pepper and possibly a pinch of salt

TO SERVE:
Whitefish roe or caviar
A few sprigs of dill and chives

Poached Salmon

Chop the carrots and slice the onions. Add the carrots, onion, water, vinegar, spices, bay leaves, bouillon, and chives to a pot. Bring to a boil and cook for 10 minutes. Cut the salmon into four equally sized pieces and place them skin side down in a container large enough to fit the bouillon. Pour the bouillon over the fish so that it is completely covered. Cover with aluminum foil and let the salmon sit in the bouillon until it has cooled. If you have time, let it sit for another couple of hours in the fridge.

It is nice to garnish with the vegetables from the bouillon, lemon wedges, and some dill. Serve the salmon cold with red caviar sauce (see p. 22).

All midsummer food should be served with fresh potatoes and plenty of dill!

6–8 SERVINGS
2 ½ lb (1 ⅕ kg) fresh salmon fillet with the skin on
2 medium-sized carrots
2 white onions
4 ¼ cups (1 liter) water
⅓ cup (75 ml) red wine vinegar
3 ½ tsp salt
10 white peppercorns
5 cloves
2 bay leaves
1 tsp Renée Voltaire's Country Bouillon (can be bought online) or 1 vegetable stock cube
a few sprigs of dill

Crisp Summer Salad

Dressing: Mix fresh lemon juice, oil, vinegar, minced garlic, and mustard. Season to taste with herb salt and pepper. Let the dressing sit for a while to let flavors blend.

Wash all your vegetables. Dry the lettuce, preferably in a salad spinner, and cut or tear it into smaller pieces. Pick over your radishes and slice them finely. Remove the seeds from the peppers and slice them. Slice the snap peas if you prefer, but you can also leave them whole. Spread the lettuce over a nice platter, and top with all the other vegetables. Drizzle the dressing over the vegetables.

1–2 heads of lettuce, such as romaine
1 bundle of radishes
1 yellow bell pepper
1 red bell pepper
1 bundle of scallions
5 ⅓ oz (150 g) snap peas

DRESSING:
the juice from ½ lemon
4 tbsp olive oil
3 tbsp balsamic vinegar
1 garlic clove, minced
1 tbsp Dijon mustard
herb salt and pepper

Västerbotten Cheese Pie

Set your oven to 400° F (200° C).

Let your puff pastry sheets thaw. Lay them over each other, on a working surface, and use a rolling pin to make a square. Place the pastry in a 10-inch pie pan. It's okay if some of the crust is hanging over the edge of the pan.

Whisk together eggs and cream. Add the cheese and stir until you have a creamy batter. Season to taste with salt and pepper (remember that the cheese is also salty).

Bake in the middle of the oven until it is golden and the filling is firm. It takes about 25–30 minutes.

10–12 PIECES
about 14 oz (400 g) frozen puff
    pastry sheets

FILLING:
4 eggs
1 ⅔ cups (400 ml) light cream
10 ½ –14 oz (300–400 g) grated
    Västerbotten cheese, or young-aged
    Parmesan
salt and ground white pepper

The Schulmans' Pickled Herring

Bring the ingredients for the pickling mixture to a boil, and then let it cool. You could also choose to stir the ingredients together without heating them. Just make sure the sugar is dissolved. Let the mixture become really cold in the fridge.

Slice the carrot and the onion. Cut the herring into pieces and add to a bowl together with onion and carrots. Pour the pickling mixture into the bowl so that it covers the fish completely.

Let the herring sit in the fridge for at least a day. Your pickled herring will be good for a week in the fridge.

10 ½ oz (300 g) herring fillet for pickling, or salted herring fillet that has been soaked in water overnight
1 small carrot
1 red onion

PICKLING MIXTURE:
⅔ cup (150 ml) water
½ cup (100 ml) sugar
¼ cup (50 ml) white distilled vinegar, preferably 12 %
8 ground allspice corns
1 bay leaf
2 cloves
4 white peppercorns

Basil Herring

Mix mayonnaise and sour cream in a bowl. Chop the basil, and add to the bowl together with cheese, minced garlic, and oil.

Drain the herring, cut it into pieces, and stir into the mayonnaise sauce. Cover the bowl and place in the fridge for up to 24 hours.

10 ½ oz (300 g) herring fillet for pickling, or salted herring fillet that has been soaked in water overnight
½ cup (100 ml) mayonnaise
½ cup (100 ml) sour cream
1 bundle of fresh basil
½ cup (100 ml) grated Parmesan
1 garlic clove, minced
4 tbsp olive oil

Mama Stina's Red Caviar Sauce

Chop the onion finely. Mix the onion, crème fraîche, and caviar. Season to taste with salt and pepper.

Serve the sauce with poached salmon (see p. 18).

1 red onion
1 ⅓ cup (300 ml) crème fraîche
3 oz (80 g) of red whitefish roe or caviar
Salt and white pepper

White Chocolate Cheesecake with Strawberries

Add the graham crackers to your food processor and pulse until you have fine crumbs, or place them in a plastic bag and crush them with a wooden spoon.

Melt the butter and mix with the crumbs. Pour the mixture into a springform tin, and use your hands or a spoon to create an even crust. Cover and place in the fridge.

Melt the chocolate in a bowl over a pot of simmering water. Stir until it is completely melted.

Stir together the cream cheese, cream, icing sugar, and mascarpone in a large bowl. Rinse and chop the strawberries into small pieces. Add the strawberries and the zest from the lemon to the batter, and pour it into the springform tin on top of the graham cracker crust. Spread the melted chocolate over the batter.

Let the cheesecake set completely in the fridge before serving. Garnish with some ripe, halved strawberries.

6–8 SERVINGS

7 oz (200 g) graham crackers
½ cup (100 g) butter
14 oz (400 g) white chocolate
9 oz (250 g) cream cheese
1 cup (250 ml) heavy cream
2 tsp icing sugar
9 oz (250 g) mascarpone cheese
2 cups (250 g) fresh strawberries + some extra for decoration
1 lemon, preferably organic

Midsummer Snaps

STRAWBERRIES, RHUBARBS, AND VANILLA

⅔ cup (100 g) fresh strawberries
2 rhubarb stalks
1 vanilla bean (or 1 tsp vanilla extract)
1 ½ tsp unrefined sugar
3 cups (700 ml) vodka

Cut the strawberries and rhubarb into pieces. If you're using a vanilla bean, cut it lengthwise into thin slices. Place everything in a glass bottle, pour in the sugar, and add the vodka.

Let it sit for at least 2 days. If you want clear snaps, you can strain it and pour the liquid back into the bottle. We think it's pretty to leave everything inside. Serve chilled.

LEMON AND DILL

2 lemons, preferably organic
2 tbsp dill seeds
3 cups (700 ml) vodka

Wash the lemons thoroughly and strip off the yellow part of the peel with a sharp knife or vegetable peeler. Add the peel and dill seeds to a glass bottle. Add the juice from the lemons, and pour in the vodka. Let it sit for at least 2 days. Run the snaps through a strainer and pour it back in the bottle. Adding a few pieces of fresh lemon peel to the bottle is a nice touch. Serve chilled.

CHILI AND GINGER

5 chilies
1 piece of fresh ginger
1 lemon
2 tsp unrefined sugar
3 cups (700 ml) vodka

Chop two of the chilies. If you want your snaps really spicy, leave the seeds in; remove them if you want it milder. Add the chopped and whole chilies to a glass bottle. The whole chilies look great in the bottle. Peel and slice the ginger finely. Add the ginger, the sugar, and the juice from the lemon to the bottle, and then pour in the vodka.

Let the snaps sit for 2–4 days. If it is too spicy, you can dilute it with some more vodka. Serve chilled.

WILD STRAWBERRIES

about 1 cup (150 g) wild strawberries
2 tsp icing sugar
15 pink peppercorns
3 cups (700 ml) vodka

Add wild strawberries, icing sugar, and pepper to a glass bottle and pour in the vodka.

Let the snaps sit for at least 24 hours. Serve chilled.

LEMON BALM AND LIME

3 limes, preferably organic
a few sprigs of fresh lemon balm
3 cups (700 ml) vodka
1 tsp unrefined sugar

Wash the limes and cut them into wedges or small pieces. Add the limes and lemon balm to a glass bottle together with vodka and sugar.

Let the snaps sit for at least 24 hours. Serve chilled.

Not Just Rosé

Rosé is wonderful in the summer, but sometimes it is fun to do something more with it than just serve it as is, especially if you're entertaining guests. Here are some refreshing favorites of ours.

BUBBLE PUNCH

10–15 GLASSES
2 limes, preferably organic
3 ⅓ oz (100 ml) simple syrup
4 ¼ cups (520 g) raspberries, fresh or frozen
2 bottles of dry rosé (750 ml each)
2 bottles of cava or prosecco (750 ml each)
ice

Wash the limes and cut them into thin slices. Pour the syrup into a large, beautiful bowl. Add some rosé and stir until the syrup has dissolved in the wine. Add the rest of the rosé, the limes, and the raspberries. Let it sit in the fridge for about an hour.

Add the cava or prosecco before serving.

SAINT TROPEZ

rosé
Fanta, or other orange soda
ice

Fill a wine glass halfway with wine. Add ice and orange soda.

BERRY BREEZE

1 GLASS
frozen red berries, such as raspberries, strawberries, and red currants
1 ⅓ oz (40 ml) Absolut Raspberri
6 ¾ oz (200 ml) rosé
3 ⅓ (100 ml) raspberry soda, or cranberry
crushed ice

Muddle the berries in your glass. Add the vodka and rosé. Top with some ice and raspberry soda.

Take Control of Your Holiday Feasts

· *You are an adult.*

· *You do whatever you want.*

· *Make a spreadsheet of how you would like your midsummer celebration to play out. Think about what suits you best this year: how you are feeling (midsummer is one of those times of year when it's normal to be exhausted), who you want to spend it with, and what you want to eat.*

· *The imperfect is the new perfect. You go a long way with good food and a good mood. Forget about perfectly folded napkins and a newly cut lawn. Embrace the meaning of summer.*

· *If you are throwing the party, ask all your guests to bring some food. You can do the basic stuff; they can bring the extras.*

· *Don't forget to enjoy yourself!*

Breakfast for Hours

We socialize best in the morning. Maybe it's because we love eating everything breakfast related, or maybe it's because we're well rested and full of life.

We have two alternative spots for enjoying our breakfast. If the weather allows, we serve breakfast outside under the apple trees. If it's raining, we gather in Hannah's kitchen. We're still half asleep with tousled morning hair, but that first cup of coffee kick-starts our engines.

Our conversations are always a certain way in the morning. They're similar to the breakfast itself—a bit unorganized and without a definite beginning or end. We start a sentence one way and finish it another way. We read newspapers, interrupt each other, paint our nails, play with the kids, cry over one thing, laugh over another, and make new plans for the day and for life. Give us a table with bread, yogurt, cold cuts, cheese, and hot coffee, and we'll be there for hours. The butter is melted, the yogurt gets warm, and all the coffee is gone for sure before we leave the table to start our day.

—Amanda and Hannah

Scrumptious and Simple Loaf

Set your oven to 400° F (200° C).

Mix filmjölk and light molasses in a bowl. Chop the nuts coarsely and mix with the dry ingredients. Mix the dry and wet ingredients.

Pour the batter into a round or rectangular loaf tin. Top with rolled oats and some chopped nuts (optional). Bake for about 40 minutes.

1 LOAF

2 cups (450 ml) filmjölk (available at Whole Foods or specialty stores), or cultured butter milk
½ cup (100 ml) light molasses
¼ cup (30 g) chopped hazelnuts
¼ cup (30 g) chopped walnuts
½ cup (50 g) cracked wheat
½ cup (50 g) crushed rye grains
⅔ cup (75 g) rolled oats
1 cup (110 g) rye flour
1 ⅓ cups (160 g) spelt flour
½ cup (60 g) flaxseeds
1 ½ tsp salt
1 ½ tsp baking powder
1 ½ tsp baking soda

Spelt Flour Scones

Set your oven to 400° F (250° C).

Cut your butter into small pieces in a bowl. Add flour, baking powder, and salt, and mix well using your fingers. Add the milk and mix until the dough is smooth.

Cut the dough into four pieces and place them on a baking sheet lined with parchment paper. Press on them with lightly floured hands to make round cakes. Cut a cross in each cake and bake in the middle of the oven for about 12 minutes.

4 SCONES

7 oz (125 g) butter
2 ½ cups (320 g) sieved spelt flour
1 cup (110 g) wholemeal spelt flour
4 tsp baking powder
1 tsp salt
1 ⅓ cups (300 ml) 2% milk

Fresh Cream Cheese

We like our cream cheese best as is, but if you prefer, you can flavor it with chives, horseradish, or black pepper.

Heat filmjölk slowly, stirring continuously, until it reaches 122° F (50° C). Remove from the heat and add the sour cream.

Pour the mix through a sieve lined with cheese cloth, a coffee filter, a thin kitchen towel, or even a few layers of paper towels. Let it drain in the fridge for
four hours.

4 ¼ cups (1 l) filmjölk (available at Whole Foods or specialty stores), or cultured butter milk
1 ⅓ cups (300 ml) sour cream

Orange & Ginger Marmalade

Wash the lemon thoroughly and cut it into thin slices. Peel the ginger and dice it finely.

Wash the oranges thoroughly. Cut each orange into four wedges and then slice them finely. Mix oranges, lemon, ginger, and sugar in a large pot. Let it sit overnight so that the fruits start to release their juices. Heat slowly and leave to simmer for 20 minutes, until the oranges are mushy.

Raise the temperature on your stove slightly and cook for another 40 minutes, until the mixture is good and sticky. Stir often so that it doesn't burn and skim off the orange foam frequently.

Pour the marmalade into clean, warm cans; close with a lid and let them cool. Store the marmalade in the fridge.

2 ¼ lb (1 kg) oranges, preferably organic
1 lemon, preferably organic
2 inches (5 cm) fresh ginger
5 cups (1 kg) sugar

Our Homemade Muesli with Coconut

Set your oven to 400° F (200° C).

Mix the nuts with the rye, spelt, seeds, and salt. Mix juice, honey, and oil and pour into the dry ingredients. Mix well.

Pour the mix into an ovenproof pan and roast in the oven for about 30 minutes. Stir it a few times so that it doesn't burn.

Let the muesli cool, and then add figs, berries, raisins, and coconut. Store the muesli in an airtight container for up to 2 weeks.

½ cup (60 g) chopped nuts, such as walnuts and hazelnuts
2 cups (215 g) rolled spelt
2 cups (215 g) rolled rye
½ cup (60 g) flaxseeds
½ cup (60 g) sesame seeds
1 tsp salt
¾ cup (200 ml) apple juice
½ (100 ml) cup honey
¼ cup (50 ml) canola oil
⅔ cup (95 g) dried figs, or other dried fruit
½ cup (65 g) dried cranberries or blueberries
⅔ cup (95 g) raisins
½ cup (40 g) coconut flakes

The World's Easiest Muesli

Chop hazelnuts and walnuts coarsely. Cut the apricots into smaller pieces. Mix all the ingredients in a bowl, and then pour into a nice jar. You can keep adding ingredients throughout the summer. We prefer to use organic ingredients, as they taste better.

½ cup (60 g) hazelnuts
½ cup (60 g) walnuts
½ cup (65 g) dried apricots
2 cups (215 g) rolled oats
2 cups (60 g) cornflakes
½ cup (65 g) raisins
½ cup (65 g) dried pineapple chunks

Beach Picnic

How to Pack the Perfect Picnic Basket

Purchase a really good cooler.

Plastic bottles, old cans, and other containers are the picnic expert's best friend. Pack your food in whatever you have on hand.

At every picnic there should be a little bit of everything, from sandwiches to fruit, to cookies, to something heartier. And, of course, a generous number of beverages!

Buy plastic bags, aluminum foil, Saran wrap, and paper plates. Being prepared with all the picnic essentials makes it so much easier.

You want the food to stay fresh for as long as possible, so bring salad dressing along on the side and pour it on your salad when it's time to eat, and make your sandwiches once you're there. Pack everything in separate containers and assemble on the spot. Everything tastes better that way!

Blankets! Bring several with you. Make sure they are easy to clean so that it doesn't matter if someone spills.

Bring napkins. Wet towels are also great to have around at the beach. And don't forget a plastic bag to throw your garbage in!

Veggies & Dip

Boil the eggs, rinse them in cold water, and let them cool.

Cut your vegetables into large pieces and put them in bowls that you can bring to the beach.

Mix crème fraîche with vegetable stock, and season to taste with lemon pepper.

Mixed vegetables, such as cauliflower, carrots, cucumber, and radishes
1 egg per person

DIP:
¾ cup (200 ml) crème fraîche
1 tbsp strong vegetable stock
2 tsp lemon pepper seasoning, or black pepper and a pinch of lemon zest

The Perfect Beach Refreshment

Add the juice from the lemon and the orange to a bottle or thermos. Add the mineral water and chopped mint. Add some orange and lemon wedges if you like. Keep it in the fridge until it's time to leave.

For a sweeter version, you can switch the mineral water for Sprite or ginger ale.

1 lemon
1 orange
6 ⅓ cup (1 ½ l) mineral water
a handful of fresh chopped mint
optional: ½ lemon, preferably organic
optional: ½ orange, preferably organic

Gazpacho

Remove the seeds from the pepper and the tomatoes, and chop them coarsely. Chop onion and garlic finely. Peel the cucumber. Add all the ingredients to a food processor and pulse until smooth. Let it sit in the fridge until it's time to leave.

Place a thermos with cold water in the fridge until it's time to leave. It will be cold and perfect for keeping your soup cool at the beach.

1 red bell pepper
4 tomatoes
1 shallot
2 garlic cloves
½ cucumber
a handful of fresh basil
1 ⅔ cup (400 ml) cold vegetable stock
½ tsp salt
a pinch of sugar
1 tsp lemon juice
freshly ground black pepper
Tabasco to taste

Mom's Chicken Salad

Boil the potatoes and let them cool. Cut the potatoes into smaller pieces. Peel and cut the eggs in half.

Pick the meat off the grilled chicken and tear or chop it into small pieces. Cook the peas according to the instructions on the package. Chop tomatoes and cucumber finely. Mix all the ingredients in a bowl.

Drizzle the salad generously with olive oil and vinegar, and season to taste with salad seasoning and herb salt. Mix well.

4 SERVINGS
1 grilled chicken
6–8 new potatoes
4 hard-boiled eggs
⅔ cup (90 g) green peas
½ cucumber
9 oz (250 g) cherry tomatoes, or
    regular
2 cups mâche lettuce

VINAIGRETTE:
3 ½ tbsp olive oil
1–2 tbsp balsamic vinegar
Italian salad seasoning
herb salt

Fried Egg & Bologna Sandwich

Fry the eggs, and turn them over to make them crispy on both sides. Fry the bologna until crisp. Split the rolls in half and fry them quickly on the cut sides if you like. Layer the bologna and egg between the bread slices, and wrap the sandwich in Saran wrap.

4 SANDWICHES
4 eggs
8 slices of Swedish Falukorv, or other
    lightly smoked bologna
butter for frying
4 bread rolls (see recipe on p. 63)

Mini Raspberry Muffins

Set your oven to 400° F (200° C).

Beat butter, vanilla extract, and sugar together until smooth. Keep beating and add the eggs, one at a time. Add the crème fraîche. Mix flour and baking powder, and add to the wet ingredients.

Line a cupcake tin with paper cupcake cups. Layer the batter with raspberries in the paper cups. Bake in the middle of the oven for 12–15 minutes. Let the muffins cool before removing them from the tin.

ABOUT 12 MUFFINS:
2 ⅔ oz (75 g) room-temperature butter
⅔ cup (120 g) sugar
2 eggs
1 ½ tsp vanilla extract
½ cup (100 ml) crème fraîche
1 ⅓ cups (180 g) all-purpose flour
1 ½ tsp baking powder
1 ¼ cups (160 g) raspberries,
    fresh or frozen

After the Sauna

We are lucky enough to have a wood-burning sauna at our country home. We Northerners adore the heat—probably because of the contrast to our cold climate. Even though our homes are always warm and cozy, the heat of the sauna still feels like a luxury.

Something about the sauna makes our conversations different. Perhaps it is because we're sitting there next to each other, warm and relaxed. Or it might be because we feel pampered and happy. Maybe it is simply the fact that we are squeezed together inside a tiny room. Sometimes we don't speak at all; we just sit there quietly. We listen to the fire pop and crackle, and the heat bites our skin. In those moments when you place the birch twigs on the hot stones, and the primeval fragrance of summer fills the whole room, there's no need to talk. You can't. Just sit there and enjoy that magical moment.

When it gets too hot, we go outside for an ice-cold rinse in the hidden shower between the apple trees. We wrap ourselves in towels, sit on the small deck in front of the sauna, open some cold beers, and treat ourselves to some cold cuts and appetizers before dinner.

—Hannah and Amanda

Chili

Cut the meat into pieces about 1 inch (2 cm) thick. Brown it in a frying pan with some butter, and then transfer it to a large stew pot. Pour a bit of water into the frying pan and then into the pot, to get all the flavors in there.

Chop the onions and bacon; sauté them in the frying pan and add them to the pot. Add enough beer and wine to cover the meat. Seed and chop the jalapeño. Add the jalapeño, chipotle paste, chili, chopped garlic, tomato purée, oregano, cumin, and salt.

Bring the stew to a boil and then lower the heat. Add a lid and leave the stew to simmer for at least 2 hours—the longer the better. Add more beer and wine as the liquid evaporates. When the meat is so tender it's starting to fall apart, it is ready to serve.

Serve with salsa, guacamole (see recipes on p. 53), and sour cream.

7–8 SERVINGS

3 ⅓ lb (1 ½ kg) chuck steak
butter for frying
3 yellow onions
5 oz (140 g) bacon
1 bottle Murphy's Irish Stout, or other
    dark beer (about 2 cups; 500 ml)
1 bottle red wine (about 3 cups; 750 ml)
2 jalapeños
2 tbsp chipotle paste
2 tbsp chili flakes
3 garlic cloves
2 tbsp tomato purée
½ tsp dry oregano
½ tsp ground cumin
salt

TO SERVE:
guacamole
salsa
sour cream

Guacamole

Split the avocados and remove the pits. Mash the avocado meat in a bowl. Finely chop the onion. Seed and finely chop the chili. Mix the avocados with onion and crème fraîche, then add minced garlic and lime juice. Season to taste with chili, salt, and pepper.

3 avocados
½ pearl onion, or shallot
1 fresh chili
½ cup (100 ml) crème fraîche
2 garlic cloves
½ lime
salt and pepper

Salsa

Chop tomatoes, onion, and garlic finely and mix them with the oil. Chop the coriander roughly and add to the salsa. Season to taste with salt and pepper.

3 tomatoes
1 yellow onion
2 garlic cloves
2 tbsp olive oil
1 bundle of fresh cilantro
½ tsp salt
a pinch of black pepper

Gustav's Playlist

Tenuousness – Andrew Bird
Behind the Moon – Matt Costa
It Will Follow the Rain – The Tallest Man on Earth
The Swimming Song – Loudon Wainwright III
Good Times – Eric Burdon & The Animals
Sacred Heart – Cass McCombs
Mathar – Dave Pike Set
Ethanopium – Dengue Fever
A Message to You, Rudy – The Specials
Hell – Squirrel Nut Zippers

Mini Guide for Cheese & Cold Cuts

What you choose to put on your cheese platter is a matter of personal taste, of course. Try as many cheeses and cold cuts as you can, until you find your favorites.

These things always have a place on our platter:
radishes
sea salt
washed-rind cheeses, preferably a strong one and a milder one, like an Epoisses and a Taleggio
Brie de Meaux
fig jam
truffle salami
fennel salumi

Also try:
Coulommiers, Brie de Meaux's more flavorful cousin
Lardo, cured pig fat
ventricina piccante, a spicy salami

Don't forget to let your cheeses sit at room temperature for at least an hour before serving. Enjoy your delicacies with beer, such as Staropramen or Corona.

Love to Bake

I only ever bake when we are in the country. Okay, I might throw together the occasional Bundt cake in the city, but that's it. It's both because I simply don't have time, and because I've started associating baking with being in my country home. When we first got our country house, there was this family living in the house next door. They were real farmers. The mom spent practically all her time baking. No bread in the history of the world can measure up to hers. Once a month all the women from the nearby farms and houses gathered in her house for "baking day." It took days to bake her bread. The flour got scalded in hot water; the dough raised twice, got infused with spices, and was then baked in the wood-burning oven, which the men had been pre-heating since early morning. You could bake 25 loaves at a time in that oven. They also made old-fashioned wafers, simple buns, cinnamon buns, and all kinds of cookies.

I should bake more often. Nothing beats fresh-baked goods. Plus working with your hands is good for you. It makes me feel happy. In our country home, I bake cinnamon buns, bread, and cookies. And I'm planning to give old-fashioned wafers a try soon. I just need to find a traditional Scandinavian wafer iron first.

—Hannah

Cardamom Cake

Set your oven to 350° F (175° C).

Melt the butter and mix it with the sugar. Add the egg and the cardamom. Mix the flour and baking powder. Add the dry ingredients and the milk to the butter and sugar a little at a time to make a smooth batter.

Grease a baking tin and sprinkle it with flour. Pour the batter into the tin and top with pearl sugar. Bake in the lower part of the oven for about 45 minutes. Do a fork test to see when the cake is ready. Let it cool on a cooling rack.

Serve the cake with whipped cream and strawberries.

¾ cup (100 g) butter
1 ¼ cups (250 g) unrefined sugar
1 egg
1 tbsp crushed cardamom seeds
2 cups (260 g) all-purpose flour
2 tsp baking powder
1 cup (250 ml) milk
butter and flour for the
    baking tin
3 tbsp pearl sugar

Grandma Gunny's Caramel Cookies

Set your oven to 400° F (200° C).

First, mix butter, sugar, and syrup. Add all the other ingredients and knead until the dough is smooth. Split the dough into three pieces. Make three rolls, place them on a baking sheet lined with parchment paper, and press on them to make them flat. Bake for about 18 minutes.

Cut the lengths diagonally while they're still hot, and then leave them to cool. (See the picture on p. 60.)

ABOUT 25 COOKIES
1 ⅔ cups (200 g) room-temperature
    butter
¾ cup (170 g) sugar
2 tbsp golden syrup, or corn syrup
1 ¾ cups (210 g) all-purpose flour
1 tsp baking soda
1 tsp vanilla extract
1 tsp ground ginger

Our Bread Rolls for the Beach

Crumble the cake yeast in a bowl. Melt the butter and mix it with the milk. Check with a candy thermometer to see that the mixture is 98° F (37° C). Pour the mixture over the yeast and stir until it's dissolved.

Add the syrup, salt, and flour. Knead the dough by hand or by using a bread mixer with dough hooks. The dough is ready when it no longer sticks to the bowl. Cover the bowl and let the dough rise for about 45 minutes.

Put the dough on a floured work surface and split it in four. Then split each of the four pieces into four again. Shape into round rolls and place on a baking sheet covered in parchment paper. Brush the rolls with egg and top with walnuts. Press the nuts halfway into the dough. Let the rolls rise for another half-hour.

Heat your oven to 400° F (200° C). Bake in the middle of the oven for about 20 minutes. (See picture on p. 61.)

16 ROLLS

1 ¾ oz (50 g) cake yeast

¼ cup (50 g) butter

2 cups (500 ml) milk

½ cup (100 ml) golden syrup, or corn syrup

2 tsp salt

5 ½–6 cups (685–740 g) all-purpose flour

beaten egg

about ½ cup (70 g) roughly chopped walnuts

Fruit & Nut Loaf

Set your oven to 400° F (200° C).

Toast nuts and almonds in a dry pan, and then let them cool. Chop figs and apricots. Mix nuts, almonds, and dried fruit with yogurt and syrup in a large bowl.

Mix flour, salt, and baking soda in another bowl, and then add them to the yogurt and fruit mix. Mix well, but not too much. The dough should be sticky.

Grease two loaf pans and sprinkle them with sunflower seeds. Divide the dough in the pans and make sure the surfaces are even. Sprinkle with some rye flour.

Bake in the middle of the oven for about an hour, then lower the heat to 350° F (175° C) and bake for another half-hour. Let the loaves cool in the loaf pans.

2 LOAVES

¾ cup (120 g) hazelnuts, walnuts, and almonds

¾ cup (100 g) dried apricots and figs

¾ cup (100 g) raisins

2 ¼ cups (1,000 ml) yogurt

¾ cup (246 g) light molasses

3 cups (370 g) all-purpose flour

1 ⅓ cups (160 g) graham flour

½ cup (86 g) rye flour

2 tsp salt

2 tsp baking soda

butter and sunflower seeds for the pans

Tapas on the Front Steps

My beloved front steps—my favorite place in the world. All my friends know what I mean when I say I need to spend some time on the steps. Here, I can just *be*. Here is also where I can enjoy a glass of wine after the kids have gone to sleep, or have important discussions over cups of coffee. If anyone asked me to name the safest place on Earth, it would probably be here. It may sound strange, but this is where I belong. If you want to get to know me, meet me here, because I'm never more myself than I am right here.

On my front steps, we meet for drinks, we have important conversations about life, and we're never interrupted. We hang out. Without expectations. The morning coffee turns into lunch, and then rosé in the afternoon sun. Often, I'm here on my own, looking out at the street that leads up to the house. It's silent, and just for me.

The front steps are also the best place for drinks before dinner. We serve our drinks with some delicious tapas.

Everyone should have their own front steps. These are mine.

—Hannah

Ceviche Bites

Season the scallops with salt and sauté them quickly in a hot pan with oil. Let them cool completely in the fridge.

Cut a cross in the tomato and add it to boiling water for 10–15 seconds. Let the tomato cool and then peel, remove seeds, and chop it finely.

Peel the shrimp. Split and remove the seed from the avocado and the mango. Chop the avocado meat, the mango, and the cucumber finely. Cut the scallion into thin slices and finely chop the red onion. Dice the cold scallops.

Remove the seeds from the chili and chop it finely. Mix chili, lime juice, minced garlic, and coriander. Add scallops, vegetables, and fruit, and season to taste with salt and pepper. Let the ceviche sit in the fridge for at least an hour.

Serve on large spoons or in shot glasses. (See picture on p. 64.)

FOR 10 SPOONS
8 large frozen scallops, thawed
1 tbsp olive oil
½ tsp salt
1 tomato
8 ¾ oz (250 g) shrimp
1 avocado
1 mango
½ cucumber
1 scallion
½ red onion
black pepper
salt

MARINADE:
1 red chili
½ lime
1 minced garlic clove
1 tbsp fresh chopped cilantro

Pimientos with Sea Salt

Pimiento de padrón is a small, green, Spanish pepper. If you can't find any, they can be substituted with small shishito peppers.

Heat the olive oil in a frying pan. Fry the peppers with sea salt until they start to soften.

20 pimientos de padrón
sea salt
olive oil

Small Potato Fritters

Peel and coarsely grate the potatoes and mix them with eggs, salt, and pepper to make a potato batter.

Add dollops of the potato batter to a hot frying pan with butter. Press down on them to flatten them, and fry on medium heat until they are crisp and golden. Let them drain for a bit on some paper towels.

To serve, place the fritters on a nice tray with a dollop of crème fraîche and some caviar on each. Top with the chopped onion.

ABOUT 10 FRITTERS
1 ½ lb (700 g) potatoes
2 eggs
1 ½ tsp salt
1 tsp black pepper
butter for frying

TO SERVE:
about ⅔ cup (100–150 ml) crème fraîche
about 3 oz (80 g) caviar
1 finely chopped red onion

Mini Bruschetta

Slice the baguette. Rub each slice with some olive oil and a garlic clove and sauté them in a frying pan, or in the oven.

Dice the tomatoes and place them in a bowl. Chop the parsley and the mozzarella. Add two minced garlic cloves, parsley, and mozzarella to the tomatoes, and season to taste with salt, pepper, and olive oil.

Place the baguette slices on a platter, and top them with the salsa and a sprinkle of sea salt.

1 sourdough baguette
olive oil
3 garlic cloves
4 tomatoes
1 bundle of fresh parsley
about 9 oz (250 g) mozzarella, preferably buffalo
sea salt and pepper

Wonderful Aperitifs

LIME GIN & TONIC

1 DRINK
1⅓ oz (40 ml) gin
2 lime wedges, preferably organic
ice
tonic water

Pour the gin into a glass. Add the lime wedges,
pressing some of their juice into the glass first. Add
ice, and top with tonic water.

PIMMS

⅓ cucumber
2 apples
2 nectarines
ice
1 bottle of Pimms No. 1 (700 ml)
about 3 cups (700 ml) ginger ale, or Sprite
a few sprigs of mint (optional)

Slice the cucumber lengthwise. Remove the pits and
seeds from the fruit and cut them into wedges. Put the
cucumber and fruit in a large pitcher with ice.

Pour Pimms and ginger ale into the pitcher, and
garnish with a few sprigs of mint if you like.

PROSECCO ROYAL

6 GLASSES
Elderberry juice (see p. 138)
1 bottle of prosecco (750 ml)

Chill the prosecco well. Pour a bit of elderberry juice
into each glass, and top with prosecco.

APPLETINI

2 DRINKS
ice
1 ⅓ oz (40 ml) vodka
1 ⅓ oz (40 ml) Sourz Sour Apple
about ½ cup (200 ml) apple juice
2 lime wedges
2 thin apple slices

Use a shaker if you have one. If not, you can use a
tall glass to shake your drinks. To give your drink a
professional touch, chill your martini glasses in the
freezer for a bit before using.

Add ice to your shaker so that it becomes cold. Pour
in vodka, Sourz Sour Apple, and apple juice. Shake
vigorously. Add the juice from the lime wedges and
shake again. Pour into martini glasses and garnish
with apple slices.

Birthday Party on the Beach

Growing up in a family with three sisters meant birthdays were really important. We were constantly competing about everything, but on birthdays things were different. An entire day belonged to the birthday girl. When it was my birthday, I knew that every second of it was mine, and I took full advantage of that fact.

I lay awake in bed in the morning, listening to the soft sounds coming from the kitchen—bread popping out of the toaster, the clinking of cups and plates, the whispering voices of my family members as they lined up outside my room ready to sing "Happy Birthday." I pretended to be asleep when they came in to wake me. They brought me breakfast in bed, flowers, and presents.

We celebrate our summer-born children at the beach. We carefully pack up home-made cake, cookies, and other goodies. We also bring tons of blankets, balloons, presents, and everything else needed for a beach birthday party.

—Amanda

Baked Saffron Pancakes

Set your oven to 350° F (175° C). Chop the almonds finely.

Add almonds, cream, eggs, and vanilla extract to the rice pudding. Mix saffron and sugar and add to the batter. Pour the batter into an ovenproof pan and bake for about 20 minutes.

Cut the pancake into pieces and serve with whipped cream and dewberry jam.

6-8 SERVINGS
2 ¼ cups (1 l) rice pudding, store-bought or homemade
½ cup (60 g) almonds, blanched
⅔ cup (150 ml) whipping cream
3 eggs
1 tsp vanilla extract
1 packet (½ g) saffron
3 tbsp sugar
butter for the pan

whipped cream
dewberry jam

Dewberry Jam

Mix the dewberries with the sugar in a stainless steel pot. Let them sit overnight.

Bring the berries and sugar to a boil. Skim off the foam, and let the mix simmer for 15 minutes. Pour the jam into clean glass jars, add lids, and let cool. Store in the fridge.

2 ¼ lb (1 kg) dewberries, or blackberries
2 ¼ lb (1 kg) sugar

Rhubarb Thumbprints

Set your oven to 350° F (175° C).

Mix butter, sugar, baking powder, and flour to make the dough. Shape the dough into fifteen balls and place each in a paper muffin cup. Use your thumb to make a dent in each of them, but don't make a hole all the way through. Add a dollop of jam to each dent.

Bake in the oven for about 15 minutes, and then let cool. (See picture on p. 77.)

15 COOKIES
¾ cup (200 g) room-temperature butter
½ cup (85 g) sugar
½ tsp baking powder
2 cups (265 g) all-purpose flour
½ cup (140 g) rhubarb jam, or rhubarb & strawberry compote (see p. 140)

Coconut Macaroons

Set your oven to 350° F (175° C).

Melt the butter and let it sit for a little bit. Mix it with all the other ingredients and let the batter sit for another 5 minutes.

Place dollops of the batter on a baking sheet lined with parchment paper. You can also shape the batter into peaks with your hands if you want, or you can place the dollops in muffin cups instead of using parchment paper. Bake for about 12 minutes. The macaroons will become firm as they cool.

ABOUT 20 MACAROONS
¼ cup (50 g) butter
2 eggs
⅔ cup (145 g) sugar
2 ⅓ cups (175 g) grated coconut

Choose Your Fillings Birthday Cake

Set your oven to 350° F (175° C).

Beat eggs and sugar until they're fluffy. Mix the dry ingredients well with a fork, and then add them to the batter. Mix until the batter is smooth, but not too smooth.

Grease and sprinkle a round, 9 inch (23 cm) baking tin with flour. Pour the batter into the tin. Bake in the lower part of the oven for about 45–50 minutes. Let the cake cool, and then cut it to make three layers.

We chose these fillings for our Charlie's birthday: custard, crushed berries, and mashed banana mixed with some whipped cream for the first layer. We added the second cake layer and then crushed meringue mixed with some whipped cream and fruit purée. Then we added the last layer of cake and covered the whole cake with whipped cream. Decorate the cake with pretty things, such as marzipan figures, sprinkles, berries . . . whatever the birthday boy or girl asks for.

THE CAKE:
5 eggs
¾ cup (170 g) sugar
½ cup (70 g) potato flour or ¾ cup
    potato flakes
½ cup (50 g) all-purpose flour
2–3 tsp baking powder
butter and flour for the
    cake tin

FILLINGS WE LOVE!
¾ cup (200 ml) thick custard
4 ¼ cups (600 g) berries
1 banana
1 ½–2 cups whipped cream
crushed meringue
1 tube of Ella's Kitchen peach & banana
    purée

Endless Barbecues

Summer sweeps through my memories. It is a steady flow of sunny days at the beach—some of them short, others lasting until dinner time. The rainy days are so extreme that we can't leave the house. But I remember our dinners best of all. They are the thread that strings together our nightly memoires of being with family and unexpected guests, and of incredible food experiences—for example, when our neighbor found truffles in his garden, or when Amanda and Alex grilled monkfish on the barbecue without gutting them first. Sometimes we dress up, but most of the time we don't. We like to keep things casual. And as long as it doesn't rain, we'd rather dress warm than stay inside.

Someone lights the outdoor fire basket. There on the patio, we talk about renovating. We discuss building a greenhouse with a dining area and infrared heaters. "When we get rich," we start, and we conclude by thinking of all the things we would do if we had a million dollars. This quickly moves us on to some fun dinner games. "The sun and the black hole" is a game where we all share what makes us happy and what makes us sad. We quiz each other, play charades, and give speeches. The guys are always embarrassed by us when we get too serious and formal, talking about all the beautiful things we love and shedding a few tears. The kids get tired after awhile, so we tuck them in under a blanket with a movie. All of this happens outside.

Yes, these barbecues really do go on forever. And they're good, fun, and essential. During the darker months, when stews simmer on our stoves and winter rambles through the city streets, we always remember these summer evenings.

—Hannah

Marinades

The marinades are all calculated for 1–1 ⅓ lb (500–600 g) of meat, and are all made the same way. Mix all the ingredients, put the meat/poultry/fish in the marinade, and let it sit in the fridge for at least 40 minutes (preferably longer). If the marinade doesn't completely cover your meat, turn it over a couple of times. The best way to do this is to put everything in a sealed plastic bag.

LAMB MARINADE

½ cup (100 ml) olive oil
2 tbsp soy sauce
1 tbsp honey
fresh rosemary
fresh thyme
salt and black pepper

PORK TENDERLOIN MARINADE

½ cup (100 ml) olive oil
1 tsp Sambal Oelek
2 tbsp concentrated veal stock, or 1 beef
  bouillon cube
2 tsp raw sugar
½ cup (100 ml) red wine
salt and pepper

SALMON MARINADE

the juice from 1 lemon
1 finely chopped chili, without seeds
2 chopped garlic cloves
a dash of white wine
½ cup (100 ml) olive oil
fresh tarragon
salt and pepper

CHICKEN MARINADE

the juice and grated zest from 2 limes
1-inch piece of ginger, peeled and grated
1 finely chopped chili, without seeds
2 garlic cloves, chopped
olive oil
salt and black pepper (optional)

JERK CHICKEN MARINADE

1 finely chopped yellow onion
2 garlic cloves, chopped
2 finely chopped chilies, without seeds
3–4 tsp ground ginger
2 tsp dried thyme
2 tsp cayenne pepper
2 tsp ground allspice
2 tsp ground cinnamon
1 tsp ground nutmeg
1 tsp salt
¼–½ cup (50 ml–100 ml) olive oil

Amelia's Parmesan Potatoes

Scrub the potatoes thoroughly, and then boil them in salted water. Grate the cheese.

Put the hot potatoes in a bowl and pour in the olive oil. Add the minced garlic and Parmesan. Mix everything well and season to taste with salt and pepper.

5–7 SERVINGS
2 ¼ lb (1 kg) new potatoes
5 ⅓ oz (150 g) Parmesan cheese
¼ cup (100 ml) olive oil
3 garlic cloves
salt and pepper

Sauces

FETA DIP

5 ⅓ oz (150 g) feta cheese
¾ cup (200 ml) crème fraîche
black pepper and sea salt

Crumble the feta cheese and mix with the crème fraîche in a nice bowl. Season to taste with pepper and salt (optional).

KOKOTOS TSATSIKI

½ cucumber, peeled and without seeds
½ tsp salt
¾ cup (200 ml) yogurt
1 garlic clove, minced
1 tsp white wine vinegar
salt and pepper

Grate the cucumber, and place it in a fine sieve with the salt to drain. Mix cucumber, yogurt, minced garlic, and vinegar. Season to taste with salt and pepper.

SAUCE WIDELL

¾ cup (200 ml) yogurt or crème fraîche
¼ cup (100 ml) concentrated veal stock, or 5 beef bouillon cubes mixed with ¼ cup of water in a food processor
2 garlic cloves, minced

Mix yogurt and veal stock, and add minced garlic. Done!

SAUCE SCHULMAN

¼ cup (100 ml) mayonnaise
¼ cup (100 ml) crème fraîche
2 tbsp tomato puree
1 tsp ketchup
1 garlic clove, minced
herb salt
paprika

Mix mayonnaise, crème fraîche, tomato purée, ketchup, and minced garlic. Season to taste with herb salt and paprika.

(See picture on p. 80.)

Lukewarm Beet & Chèvre Salad

Boil the beets in a large pot. It is hard to say how long it will take, as it depends on the size of the beets. You know that they are done when they can be easily pierced all the way through with a fork. Pull the peels off the beets under cold water, and then chop them into smaller pieces.

Chop asparagus and beans into smaller pieces (optional). Sauté them in a frying pan with olive oil together with the nuts.

Spread the arugula and spinach over a large serving plate in a bowl. Top with beets, asparagus, beans, and nuts. Break the chèvre into smaller pieces and add to the salad.

Vinaigrette: Mix oil, balsamic cream, and honey. Season to taste with salad seasoning, herb salt, and pepper.

Drizzle the salad with the vinaigrette.

8–10 SERVINGS

2 ¼ lb (1 kg) beets
9 oz (250 g) asparagus
3 ½ oz (100 g) green beans, such as haricots verts
½ cup (50 g) pine nuts or hazelnuts
olive oil for frying
3 ½ cups (70 g) arugula
3 ½ cups (70 g) baby spinach
½ lb. (250 g) chèvre (fresh, soft goat cheese)

VINAIGRETTE:

¼ cup (100 ml) olive oil
2 tbsp balsamic cream
1 tbsp honey
Italian salad seasoning
herb salt
black pepper

Luxury Bananas Grilled in Foil

Slice the bananas open lengthwise (without removing the peel) and stuff them full of chocolate. Choose your favorite chocolate. Wrap the bananas in aluminum foil and grill on your barbecue for about 15 minutes.

Serve the bananas and chocolate with ice cream.

4 SERVINGS
4 bananas
3 ½ oz (100 g) mint chocolate
3 ½ oz (100 g) chocolate with nuts
3 ½ oz (100 g) candy cane chocolate
  (or more mint chocolate)

TO SERVE:
vanilla ice cream

A Rainy Day

The rainy days. They help us pull ourselves together a bit. They're important. To be perfectly honest, I think the rainy days are what really prepare us and give us energy to take on the fall. They force us to go inside, do things slowly, just stop everything, and relax. The rain used to depress me. Now I see it as an opportunity to just *be*. We play games, bake some cinnamon rolls, and laugh. We also take this opportunity to take naps. We draw and make crafts, and I take in all the wonderful thoughts and ideas that the children come up with. I love having all the cousins gathered at the kitchen table, waiting for pancakes, having hilarious conversations, and fighting over crayons. These are the moments that count. When our kids grow up, these will be their safe and happy childhood memories.

—Hannah

Cardamom Rolls
& Blueberry Rolls

It is easiest to make the dough in a dough mixer, but you can also make it by hand.

Melt the butter, add the milk, and let it cool down to a lukewarm temperature—approximately 98° F (37° C). Crumble the yeast in a large bowl (or the bowl of the dough mixer). Pour the butter and milk over the yeast and mix until there are no lumps.

Add sugar, eggs, cardamom, and salt. Then add the flour, a little at a time. Mix until the dough is smooth. You know it's ready when it has a glossy finish, and doesn't stick to the bowl. Cover the bowl with a towel and let the dough rise for 1 hour.

Beat together the ingredients for filling 2 with an electric mixer.

Split the dough in four, and work with one piece at a time on a floured work surface. Use a rolling pin to create rectangles. Spread the filling out evenly and roll the dough up to create logs. Cut them into 1¼ inch (3–4 cm) thick slices, put them cut side up in paper muffin cups, and place them on baking sheets. Fill half of the rolls with jam, and half with cardamom filling. Cover the rolls with towels and let them rise for about half an hour.

Brush the rolls with egg. Sprinkle the blueberry rolls with pearl sugar, and the cardamom rolls with cardamom seeds. Bake in the middle of a 440° F (225° C) oven until they are golden. It takes about 8–10 minutes.

ABOUT 60 ROLLS
¾ cup (200 g) butter
4 ¼ cup (1 l) milk
1 ¾ oz (50 g) cake yeast
¾ cup (170 g) sugar
2 eggs
1 tsp ground cardamom
a pinch of salt
about 12 cups (1 ½ kg) all-purpose
    flour

FILLING 1:
1 ¼ cup (400 g) blueberry jam

FILLING 2:
1 ⅓ cup (300 g) butter, room
    temperature
3 tbsp ground cardamom
¾ cup (170 g) sugar
1 tbsp vanilla extract
2 tbsp golden syrup, or corn syrup

TOPPINGS
1 beaten egg
pearl sugar
crushed cardamom seeds

Asparagus Carbonara

Start by bringing a large pot of generously salted water to a boil. Cook the pasta according to the instructions on the package.

Dice the bacon and finely chop the onion. Sauté the bacon and onion, and chop the asparagus. Once the bacon is crispy, add the asparagus.

Mix the eggs, cream, cheese, finely chopped garlic, salt, and pepper in a bowl to make a "cream sauce."

Pour the drained pasta into the frying pan with the bacon, onion, and asparagus, and lower the heat. Add the cream sauce and stir.

Serve your carbonara on a large platter or in a nice bowl, season with freshly ground pepper, and top with some more grated Parmesan.

4 SERVINGS
14 oz (400 g) pasta
10 oz (280 g) bacon
1 yellow onion
9 oz (250 g) asparagus, fresh or frozen and thawed
4 eggs
⅔ cup (150 ml) heavy cream
3 ½ oz (100 g) Parmesan
2 garlic cloves
salt and black pepper

Pancakes with Bacon & Lingonberries

Mix flour and salt in a large bowl. Add half of the milk and beat to a smooth batter. Add the rest of the milk and the eggs. If you have the time, let the batter sit for half an hour.

Fry the pancakes in a lot of butter, and test your way to the right amount of batter and stove temperature, starting with ¼ cup of batter and medium heat.

Add a little bit of sugar to the lingonberries and stir until the sugar has dissolved. Add more sugar to taste. Fry the bacon or salted pork in a frying pan, and let it dry on some paper towels.

Serve the pancakes and bacon with lingonberries for the grown-ups, and raspberry jam for the kids.

4 SERVINGS
1 cup (130 g) all-purpose flour
½ tsp salt
2 ½ cups (600 ml) milk
3 eggs
3 tbsp butter
¾ cup (100 g) lingonberries or cran-berries, fresh or frozen and thawed
sugar
10 ½ oz bacon or sliced salted pork
raspberry jam

Creamy Veal Stew with Dill

This veal stew with dill is a little tricky, but don't let it intimidate you, because it is also the most delicious thing ever. And it's easier than you would think.

Cut the meat into 1–1 ½ inch (3–4 cm) pieces, and put it in a large stew pot. Bring the water and salt to a boil in another pot, and then pour it over the meat. Bring to a boil again. Use a ladle to skim off all the fat that rises to the surface.

Cut the carrot, onion, and leek into smaller pieces and add them to the stew together with peppercorns, bay leaves, dill seeds, dill stalks, and possibly some more salt. Add a lid and let the stew simmer on low heat for 75–90 minutes, or until the meat is really tender.

Remove the meat from the pot and keep it warm. Strain the broth and save it.

Sauce: Melt the butter. Add the flour and stir well. Add 2–2 ½ cups (500–600 ml) of the broth while whisking continuously. Let the sauce simmer until it thickens.

Add the meat to the sauce and let it simmer for 5 minutes. Stir every once in a while. Add vinegar, lemon juice, and sugar to taste. If you like, mix an egg yolk with about half a cup of cream, and add to the stew. From this point on the stew should only simmer, never boil. Add the dill, and season to taste with salt and pepper.

Serve with boiled potatoes.

8 SERVINGS
3 ⅓ lb (1 ½ kg) lamb, without bones
6 ⅓ cup (1 ½ l) water
1 ½ tsp salt
1 carrot
1 yellow onion
½ leek
10 white peppercorns
2 bay leaves
½ tsp dill seeds
the stalks from a bundle of dill

SAUCE:
2 tbsp butter
2 tbsp all-purpose flour
2–2 ½ cup (500–600 ml) broth
2 tsp white distilled vinegar (12%)
2 tbsp lemon juice
1-2 tsp sugar
1 egg yolk (optional)
about ½ cup (100–200 ml) heavy cream (optional)
½ cup finely chopped dill
salt and freshly ground white pepper

TO SERVE:
boiled potatoes

All Delicious Things at Once

There is something wonderful about making whatever delicious food you can think of. Everyone gets to choose their favorite dish, and we turn it into a buffet, or a sort of tapas dinner. It's a dream, getting to taste all of that scrumptious food: cheese, pasta, salad, and other lovely things.

It is much like the cake in this chapter, which is a mix of the two best cakes in the world: Pavlova, and the Swedish princess cake. Combine those two, and you get this unbelievably imaginative and yummy cake. This is what it looks like when we choose to eat anything and everything we want all at once.

—Amanda

Endives with Blue Cheese

Rinse the endive leaves in cold water, pat them dry, and place them on a nice platter. Add a piece of cheese and a slice of pear to each leaf. Top with walnuts.

10 endive leaves, or other lettuce
5 oz (140 g) blue cheese
2 pears
½ cup (50 g) walnuts

Pesto Pasta

Bring generously salted water to a boil in a large pot. Cook the pasta according to the instructions on the package.

Mix nuts, basil, Parmesan, garlic, and oil using a hand mixer. Add the crème fraîche, and season to taste with pepper, and possibly a bit of salt.

Mix the steaming pasta with the pesto.

4 SERVINGS
14 oz (400 g) pasta, such as tagliatelle
a large bundle of fresh basil
3 ½ oz (100 g) Parmesan
3 garlic cloves
¾ cup (200 ml) olive oil
¼ cup (50 ml) crème fraîche
salt and pepper

Prosciutto, Chèvre, & Mushroom Salad

Chop shallots and garlic. Pick over your mushrooms and chop large ones into smaller pieces. Sauté the garlic and half of the shallots in a frying pan with butter. Add mushrooms, a bit of oil, and half of the thyme. Season to taste with salt and pepper. Sauté the mushrooms until most of the liquid is gone.

Wash the tomatoes, cut them in half, and put them in a bowl together with thinly sliced ham, the rest of the shallots, pieces of chèvre, the rest of the thyme, and a bit of olive oil. Season with salt and pepper, and mix well.

Spread the mushrooms over a nice serving platter, and top with the salad.

4 SERVINGS
4 shallots
1 garlic clove
4 ½ cups (250 g) of mixed fresh mushrooms
1 tbsp butter, for frying
olive oil
2 sprigs of fresh thyme
12 cherry tomatoes
14 oz (400 g) prosciutto
3 ½ oz (100 g) chèvre
salt and pepper

Princess Cake with Meringue

Set your oven to 200°F (100° C).

Beat egg whites until firm, adding the sugar a little at a time. The classic rule of thumb for when it's ready is when you can turn the bowl upside down without the meringue sliding out.

Draw two circles on a parchment paper (these will help you make round cake bases). Pour the meringue into a large piping bag, and fill in the circles. Bake in the middle of the oven for about an hour and a half. Let the meringue cool.

Mash the strawberries, and whip the cream. Mix some of the whipped cream with the strawberries, and spread the mix over one of the meringue bases. Add the second base, and cover the whole cake in whipped cream.

Use a rolling pin to make a thin layer of marzipan, large enough to cover the cake. Place it over the cake, and cut off any edges. Sprinkle with icing sugar, and top with a real rose.

6 egg whites
1 ⅓ cup (250 g) sugar

FILLING AND TOPPING
¾ cup (150 g) fresh strawberries
3 cups (700 ml) whipping cream
18 oz (500 g) pink marzipan
icing sugar

Barbecue by the Sea

Sometimes we all need to feel like we can manage on our own, without shiny kitchen appliances and tools. I love feeling as though we know how to cook—no one can take that away from us—and knowing that we can manage by ourselves in nature.

When we go barbecuing on the beach, that's exactly how it feels. We look for the very best spot, unpack, and arrange our blankets carefully, as if we were going to stay there the whole summer. The kids look for firewood, and we build our own barbecues, cooking the meat on stones we heat in the fire. We chill our refreshments in the sea, and eat everything else as is. Food and wine have never tasted better than they do there by the sea. There is something about the empty, barren landscape that changes you as a person. It makes you feel softer and wilder. You become humble in the presence of all that stone. The stones have been there, slowly getting shaped by the sea, for tens of thousands of years, and it makes us feel strongly that we are only visitors here. We're only here for a short while.

My dearest memories from childhood are of evenings here. How I played and ate until I would fall asleep on my mother's lap to the sound of the grown-ups chattering, and the smell of the fire, coffee, red wine, and the sea. The high point of the evening was when the sun finally dropped into the sea. We could rarely stay awake long enough to see it, but that didn't matter much.

Today we do the same thing with our children. We might manage to go only once or twice a year, but when we do, we have an amazing time! The only thing missing is someone who knows how to play the guitar. We'll have to make that a project for next year.

—Amanda

Garlic Sauce

Mince the garlic cloves and mix them with the crème fraîche. Add parsley and season to taste with salt and pepper.

3 garlic cloves
⅔ cup (150 ml) crème fraîche
1 tbsp finely chopped parsley
salt and white pepper

Ajvar

Set your oven to 350° F (180° C).

Finely chop the onion and garlic and sauté them in oil. Finely chop the chili and add it to the onions and garlic for a couple of minutes. Split the peppers and remove their seeds, and then roast them in the oven for about 20 minutes.

Blend the onion mix and the peppers with some oil and vinegar in a food processor. Season to taste with salt, pepper, and a pinch of sugar. Let the ajvar cool in the fridge.

1 yellow onion
3 garlic cloves
olive oil
1 chili
2 red bell peppers
1 tbsp white wine vinegar
sugar
salt and pepper

Marinated Olives

Crumble the bay leaf and mix it with all the other ingredients in a bowl. Cover the bowl with plastic wrap and let it sit for at least a few hours, but preferably overnight.

As we are garlic lovers, we often use more than 4 cloves, but you can choose for yourself how strong you want your marinade to be.

1 ⅓ cups (240 g) black olives
1 bay leaf
4 garlic cloves
1 tbsp fresh rosemary
1 tbsp fresh oregano
2 tsp grated lime zest, preferably organic
¼ cup (50 ml) olive oil
1 tsp sea salt

Potato Salad with Radishes & Halloumi

Scrub the potatoes and boil them in salted water. Cut the halloumi into sticks and fry it in olive oil until it is browned and softened. Rinse the arugula and the radishes in water. Slice the radishes. Mix all the ingredients in a bowl and season generously with salad seasoning.

The potatoes should be lukewarm when you mix the salad. If they are very small, it is nice not to cut them at all.

Serve the potato salad with grilled sausages, their sauces, and marinated olives (see p. 114).

6–7 SERVINGS
2 ⅕ lb (1 kg) new potatoes
7–9 oz (200–250 g) halloumi cheese (can be found at Whole Foods, or other specialty stores)
3 ½ cups (70 g) arugula
a bundle of radishes
Italian salad seasoning

TO SERVE:
good sausages, such as lamb sausages or salsiccia

Flatbread Quesadillas

Add a generous spread of cream cheese to two of the flatbreads. Add a layer of pesto, and top with the remaining flatbreads. Cut into squares and grill them briefly before serving.

12 PIECES
4 slices of flatbread, or tortillas
7 oz (200 g) cream cheese
4 tbsp pesto

Sticky Chocolate Pie

Set your oven to 350° F (175° C).

Melt the butter in a pot and then remove it from the heat. Add sugar, vanilla extract, and eggs to the butter and mix well. Add flour and cocoa and stir until you have a smooth batter. Pour the batter into a greased, round 9-inch (22-cm) baking pan, dusted with flour. Top with chopped nuts if you like.

Bake for 20–25 minutes. The pie should still be soft and sticky in the middle. Serve with whipped cream.

6–8 SERVINGS
½ cup (100 g) butter
1 cup (210 g) sugar
2 eggs
⅔ cup (80 g) all-purpose flour
4 tbsp cocoa
1 ½ tsp vanilla extract
butter and flour for the pan
hazelnuts (optional)

Potluck with "Presents" on the Barbecue

Summer camp.

This was long before I got my own country home. Mom was single and had inexhaustible patience when it came to us and our friends, who all roamed the house. She brought us all together. It was as if she knew that if she didn't accept our teenage mind-set and world, we wouldn't stick around. Today, I can only thank her for coping so well with all our friends, boyfriends, love troubles, parties, hungover food orgies, and crazy drama.

During this period we always joked that mom's house was like a summer camp, or a foster home. For some reason we all hung out there. A lot of us had dysfunctional backgrounds — all telling made-up stories that were actually painfully close to the truth. There was Saga, a girl who came every summer as she had nowhere else to go. In the kitchen, Åsa, the shoplifter, used Mom's kitchen sofa as a therapy couch. There were Amanda and Amelia, who first came as babies, and never found another home. Markus was obsessed with money because he never had any . . . The games relieved us of any responsibility for a while. Mom was everyone's mom, and she had time for everyone.

I remember one summer in particular, when we spent enjoying uncountable dinners at my mom's mill. Amanda made a blueberry pie that was so good that even Micke, who had restrained from sweets for years, couldn't help himself. We left the dinner table to go for nighttime swims, and then the party continued all night long, with loud music blasting on the cassette player.

Sometimes I wish I could go back to those days. I'd like to be carefree again, and not think about things like renovating houses, running out of water, or other grown-up things. Not thinking about tomorrow, and being millions of miles away from thoughts of family and children. But it's only for a moment. Then I want to be back here and now, in this life. My life.

—Hannah

Savory Presents

Having been brought up in a bohemian environment, potlucks are nothing new for us. Potlucks, food committees—we did everything collectively. That has stuck with us. And it is the very best way to arrange a big dinner. At this potluck, dinner is taking care of itself on the barbecue, and the guests bring their own meat. We get the whole family to chop and wrap up the rest of the dinner in little aluminum foil "presents" (wraps with various fillings) beforehand, to throw on the barbecue later.

PRESENT 1

2 heads (about 18 oz) broccoli
blue cheese
walnuts
olive oil

Prepare a piece of aluminum foil for each person. Separate the broccoli into florets and divide them over the aluminum foil sheets. Add crumbled cheese and walnuts. Drizzle with a bit of oil, close the packages, and place on the barbecue.

PRESENT 2

2 ¼ lb (1 kg) small fresh potatoes
4 ½ oz (125 g) canned anchovies
1 red onion
olive oil

Prepare a piece of aluminum foil for each person. Wash the potatoes, and cut them into smaller pieces if they are big. Chop the anchovies finely and slice the onion. Divide everything over the aluminum foil sheets, and drizzle with oil. Close the packages, and place them on the barbecue.

We always use raw potatoes, but you can also use cooked or parboiled potatoes. Raw potatoes will need more time on the grill.

PRESENT 3

25 cherry tomatoes
5 ⅓ oz (150 g) feta cheese
olive oil
sea salt

Prepare a piece of aluminum foil for each person. Divide the tomatoes over the aluminum foil sheets, and add crumbled feta. Top with a drizzle of oil and a sprinkle of salt. Close the packages, and place them on the barbecue.

PRESENT 2

1 bundle of fresh red onion
1 bundle of fresh yellow onion
olive oil
sea salt

Prepare a piece of aluminum foil per person. Cut the leaves off the onions and place them whole or cut in half on the aluminum foil sheets. Top with a drizzle of oil and a sprinkle of salt. Close the packages, and place them on the barbecue.

Serve the wraps together with the meat brought by your guests. You could also ask guests to prepare one of these little presents at home, and bring that with them.

Aioli with Basil & Parmesan

Mince the garlic and mix it with the egg yolks in a bowl. Add the oil a few drops at a time while beating continuously. An electric beater is preferable. Finely chop the basil and add it to the aioli. Add the cheese, and season to taste with vinegar and salt.

6 garlic cloves
3 egg yolks
⅔ cup (150 ml) canola oil
a large bundle of fresh basil
½ cup (42 g) finely grated Parmesan
1 ½ tsp apple cider vinegar
salt

Feta Cheese Dip with Sundried Tomatoes

Drain the tomatoes. Mix the tomatoes with feta cheese, nuts, and olive oil in a food processor, until it reaches your preferred consistency. Season to taste with salt and pepper.

⅔ cup (65 g) marinated sundried tomatoes
5 ⅓ oz (150 g) feta cheese
½ cup (50 g) pine nuts
2 tbsp olive oil
salt and pepper

Yogurt Sauce with Lime & Mint

Chop the mint finely and mix with the yogurt. Add the juice from the lime. Season to taste with black pepper, Italian salad seasoning, and herb salt.

¾ cup yogurt
a large bundle of fresh mint
1 lime
black pepper
Italian salad seasoning
herb salt

Sweet Presents

STRAWBERRIES, BLUEBERRIES, AND COOKIE DOUGH

8 WRAPS

COOKIE DOUGH

7 oz (200 g) butter

½ cup (50 g) sifted spelt flour

½ cup (50 g) rolled oats

½ cup (85 g) raw sugar

1 tbsp vanilla extract

½ cup (60 g) chopped hazelnuts

4 cups (600 g) fresh strawberries

4 cups (600 g) fresh blueberries

TO SERVE:

vanilla ice cream or custard

Cut the butter into smaller pieces and mix with flour, rolled oats, and sugar. When you have a crumbly dough, add the nuts.

Prepare a piece of aluminum foil for each person. Slice the strawberries and divide them over the aluminum foil sheets together with the blueberries. Top with the cookie dough. Fold the edges of the aluminum foil to create little bowls, and put them on the barbecue toward the end, when the fire has turned into a nice bed of embers. Grill for about 10 minutes.

Serve with vanilla ice cream or a dollop of custard.

MINT CHOCOLATE PEARS

8 WRAPS

3 cans of preserved pears, 14 oz each

16 pieces of After Eight, or other mint chocolate

TO SERVE:

vanilla ice cream

Prepare a piece of aluminum foil for each person. Add two pear halves to each aluminum foil sheet, and top them with two After Eight pieces. Wrap the foil up tightly. Grill for about 10 minutes.

Serve with vanilla ice cream.

Tired of Barbecues

At the start of summer I always think I could never get tired of barbecues. But that day always arrives at some point. I suddenly don't want to lay eyes on another bag of charcoal ever again. I want to stop in the middle of the supermarket and yell, "Barbecue, I've had enough!" On those days, I don't want to be outside in the sun. I almost want to return to the city just to avoid yet another barbecue.

Almost on demand comes an evening with terrible, rainy weather, and staying indoors is inevitable anyway. We put on woolen socks and light a fire. And we cook something that we rarely make during the summer months: a really good Bolognese. Chop the ingredients carefully and slowly. There is no better time for reflection than when you're in the kitchen chopping something. I call it "chopping therapy." It's pretty nice to not have a bright sun calling you through the window to come outside.

So, open a bottle of wine, light some candles, give all of your love to this Bolognese, and sprinkle the apple pie generously with cinnamon.

—Amanda

Baked Brie

Set your oven to 400° F (200° C).

Place the cheese on a baking sheet lined with parchment paper. Cut the tomatoes into wedges, and chop the nuts roughly. Place the tomatoes and nuts on top of the cheese and top with oil and honey. Heat in the oven for 5–20 minutes.

Serve with bread. (See picture on p. 130.)

6–8 SERVINGS
1 whole brie
7 roma tomatoes
½ cup (50 g) walnuts
1 tbsp olive oil
1 tbsp honey

Bolognese

Chop the onion and sauté it in butter and olive oil, on low heat, for about 10 minutes.

Add salt, pepper, paprika, and finely chopped chili and garlic. Add the minced meat and sauté until it's cooked through. Then add tomatoes, veal stock, tomato purée, and ketchup.

The longer you let the Bolognese simmer, the better. Make sure it's at least half an hour. If it gets dry, add a little bit of water and oil. Finally, add the crème fraîche, and season to taste with salt and pepper. Serve with steaming pasta and grated Parmesan.

4–5 SERVINGS
1 yellow onion
2 tbsp (25 g) butter
2 tbsp olive oil
paprika
½ chili (leave it out if cooking for kids)
3 garlic cloves
18 oz (500 g) beef mince
18 oz crushed tomatoes
1 tbsp concentrated veal stock, or 1 beef bouillon cube
1 tbsp tomato purée
2 tbsp ketchup
2 tbsp crème fraîche
salt and pepper

TO SERVE:
pasta
Parmesan

Apple Pie

The dough for this pie is amazing! I first had it at a friend's house and just had to ask for the recipe. It turned out to be my friend's mom, Marianne's, recipe. So when I happened to run into her, I asked for it again.

A couple of weeks later, I got the most beautiful handwritten letter from her, containing the incredibly simple and delicious recipe. Since then, this is my go-to pie recipe, and I use it for apple pie, blueberry pie, raspberry pie, and any other pie you can think of.

Set your oven to 400° F (200° C).

Crust: Melt the butter in a saucepan. Add all the other ingredients to the saucepan and mix well. Press three-fourths of the dough into an ovenproof pan.

Filling: Remove the seeds from the apples, and then slice them. Chop the hazelnuts. Mix the sugar and the cinnamon. Fill the pie crust with the apples and sprinkle the nuts and sugar mixture on top. Top with the remaining dough in crumbles. Bake for about half an hour.

Serve with custard, or perhaps some cinnamon ice cream.

6 SERVINGS

CRUST:
2 ¼ cups (275 g) butter
½ cup (96 g) sugar
1 ⅓ cups (160 g) all-purpose flour
1 tsp baking powder
1 tsp salt

FILLING:
6 apples
¾ cup (100 g) hazelnuts
1 tsp ground cinnamon
2 tbsp sugar

TO SERVE:
custard or cinnamon ice cream

Cinnamon Ice Cream

This ice cream is so easy to make; it almost feels like cheating, but it is so good. Whip the cream, and mix it with the other ingredients in a plastic container with a lid. Let it set in the freezer for at least 3 hours. Take it out of the freezer about 15 minutes before it's time to serve.

4-6 SERVINGS
1 ⅔ cups (400 ml) whipping cream
¾ cup (200 ml) yogurt
2 tsp ground cinnamon
⅖ cup (96 g) sugar

Elderflower, Rhubarbs, & Plums

Miss Do-it-yourself makes her own syrups and jams . . . Preserving absolutely everything the garden offers before winter comes. That's the dream, isn't it?

I find mushroom picking to be extremely provoking. Walks in the forest and home-making . . . Sometimes I just want to shoot people who come over carrying jars for hostess gifts. You know, the glass jars with pretty handwritten tags, plaid fabric, and nice ribbons around them. Do-it-yourself hostess gifts.

Show-offs and high-hats is what they are, the syrup and jam makers. But all of this is just jealousy. There is nothing more satisfying than enjoying your own home-made applesauce, made from apples from your own tree. I love it, and I am going to become one of those annoying DIY people—starting right now.

–Hannah

Elderberry Juice

Clean a large plastic tub or bucket thoroughly. Wash the elderflower blossoms in cold water.

Bring the water, sliced lemons, citric acid, and sugar to a boil. Place the blossoms in your bucket and pour the boiling syrup over them. Cover with aluminum foil and let sit in a cool place for 4 days.

Drain the lemonade and pour it into bottles. You can also freeze it to make it keep longer. (See picture on p. 136.)

17 OUNCES (4 L)
40 elderflower blossoms
13 cups (3 l) water
4 lemons, preferably organic
2 ⅔ oz (75 g) citric acid (can be purchased at Whole Foods)
4 ⅖ lb (2 kg) sugar

Rhubarb Pie

Set your oven to 300° F (150° C).

Mix all the dry ingredients in a bowl. Melt the butter together with the cream and syrup, and pour the mix into the dry ingredients.

Peel and chop the rhubarbs. Pour the batter into a greased, ovenproof pan and spread the rhubarbs on top of it. Sprinkle the raw sugar over the rhubarbs. Bake for about 40 minutes.

Serve with vanilla ice cream.

10 SERVINGS
¾ cup (67 g) rolled oats
¾ cup (170 g) sugar
¾ cup (90 g) all-purpose flour
a few drops of vanilla extract
½ cup (125 g) butter
½ cup (50 ml) heavy cream
½ cup (50 ml) golden syrup, or corn syrup
about 1 lb (500 g) rhubarb
2 tbsp raw sugar

TO SERVE:
custard

Rhubarb & Strawberry Compote

Pick over the rhubarbs and cut it into ½ inch (1 cm) pieces. Bring water, sugar, and rhubarbs to a boil. Slice the strawberries and add them to the pot. Let it simmer until the rhubarbs and strawberries have softened.

Mix potato starch and water. Remove the pot from the heat and add the starch mix to the compote. Season with cinnamon and cardamom and let it cool.

Serve the compote warm with ice cream, or cold with yogurt in the morning.

4 SERVINGS
6 rhubarb stalks
½ cup water
¼ cup (40 g) sugar
¾ cup (130 g) fresh strawberries
½ tsp ground cinnamon
½ tsp ground cardamom

THICKENING:
2 tbsp potato starch
3 tbsp water

Blackberry & Raspberry Marmalade

Let the berries thaw if using frozen, and mash them in a saucepan. Bring them to a boil and add the sugar, a little at a time.

If you're using a vanilla bean, split it in half, scrape out the seeds and add to the marmalade. Let it simmer for about 25 minutes.

Pour the marmalade into a clean and pretty glass jar. Enjoy it with some good cheese, or on your breakfast sandwich. Store in the fridge.

7 oz (200 g) raspberries, fresh or frozen
7 oz (200 g) blackberries, fresh or frozen
¾ cup (170 g) sugar
1 vanilla bean (or 1 tsp vanilla extract)

Plum Chutney

Rinse and dice the plums, and mix them with the rest of the ingredients in a heavy-bottomed pot. Simmer without a lid for about half an hour, until the plums are soft and the mixture is sticky.

Let the chutney cool and pour it into a clean jar. The chutney goes great with all kinds of grilled meat, as well as on a cheese platter! Store in the fridge.

8 ripe plums
½ cup (100 ml) red wine
1 tbsp balsamic vinegar
½ cup (60 g) dark muscovado sugar
a pinch of salt
a pinch of cayenne pepper
2 cinnamon sticks
1 chopped garlic clove

Black Currant Jelly

Add the berries and the water to a pot and bring them to a boil. Let them simmer until the berries break apart. If they don't break, you can mash them using a wooden spoon. Pour the berry mash through a cheesecloth into a different pot. It takes about half an hour.

Throw away what's left in the cloth. Measure the liquid. Add 3 ¾ cups (760 g) of sugar per every 4 ¼ cups (1 liter) of liquid; stir and bring to a boil for about 10 minutes.

Pour the jelly into clean and warm glass jars, add lids, and let them cool. Store unopened jars in a cool place, and opened jars in the fridge.

17 OUNCES
4 ⅕ cups (625 g) black currants
1 cup (250 ml) water
3 ¾ cups gelling sugar (can be easily found on Amazon, or substituted with pectin, which can be found at most grocery stores) per 4 ¼ cups (1 l) liquid

Crayfish Feast

There is something special about our traditional crayfish feasts. When the time comes to fish for crayfish, the time has also come to round off summer. The sun that never used to set now does. The night comes faster, and the sparkling light of stars is once again visible in the August sky before dinner is over. In Sweden we often talk about how the August moon sits so low in the sky—heavy and clear—that it seems to be there as compensation for the sun. We eat our crayfish and drink our snaps below that moon and the colorful lanterns that we hang from the trees.

—Amanda

Chanterelle Salad with Aged Cheese Pesto

Chop, then sauté the shallot in oil and butter. Add the mushrooms to the shallot for a little bit. Add the vinegar and let it simmer with the mushrooms until reduced. Turn the heat off and sprinkle the mushrooms with parsley.

Split some of the tomatoes in half if you want. Separate the cabbage leaves. Rinse and dry them, tear them into smaller pieces, and spread them over a large serving platter. Add the mushrooms and tomatoes, and top with olive oil and sea salt.

Pesto: Chop the dill roughly, and then mix all the ingredients using a food processor. Add more oil if the pesto is too thick. Season to taste with salt and pepper. Store in the fridge and take it out when it's time to serve.

Add dollops of pesto on the salad, or serve it separately on the side.

4–6 SERVINGS

1 shallot
butter and olive oil
1 lb fresh chantarelles, or other wild
    mushrooms
¼ cup (50 ml) balsamic vinegar
½ cup roughly chopped parsley
10 oz (300 g) red and yellow cherry
    tomatoes
½–1 head of savoy cabbage
sea salt

DILL AND AGED CHEESE PESTO:

4 sprigs of dill
¾–1 cup (145 g) of hazelnuts and
    almonds
¾ cup (85 g) Västerbotten cheese,
    Parmesan, or other aged cheese
1 handful of arugula
2 tbsp fresh lemon juice
¾ cup (200 ml) olive oil
a pinch of salt and black pepper

Crayfish Marinade

Bring all the ingredients, except a few sprigs of dill, to a boil. Add a third of the crayfish and put a lid on the pot. As soon as it boils again, add half of the remaining crayfish. Repeat with the rest. Let them all cook for another 5 minutes. Add the reserved dill.

Let sit in a cool place for 24 hours.

FOR ABOUT 60 LIVE CRAYFISH:
1 ⅓ gallons (5 l) water
¾ cup (250 g) kosher salt
1 cup (225 ml) beer
5 sugar cubes
1–2 bundles of dill

Crab Cakes with Dill Mayo

Mix crab meat, chopped dill, mayonnaise, Tabasco, lemon juice, egg, and salt in a bowl. Let it sit in the fridge for about half an hour.

Shape the crab cake mixture into six balls and flatten them carefully. Cover the crab cakes in breadcrumbs and, still handling them carefully, fry them in butter. Serve with the dill mayo.

Dill mayo: Mince the garlic. Beat the egg yolks with the garlic, vinegar, salt, and pepper in a bowl, preferably with an electric beater. Add the oil a little at a time while beating fast and continuously. Add finely chopped dill when it's time to serve.

6 CAKES
16 oz (450 g) crab meat or imitation crab
4 sprigs of dill
1 ½ tbsp mayonnaise
1 tsp Tabasco, or more if you want more of a sting
½ lemon
1 egg
a little bit of salt
breadcrumbs
butter for frying

DILL MAYO:
3 garlic cloves
3 egg yolks
2 tsp white wine vinegar
1 ¼ cups (300 ml) canola or corn oil
a few large sprigs of dill
salt and pepper

Sticky Chocolate Pie with Blackberries

Set your oven to 350° F (175°C) .

Melt the butter and remove from the heat. Add sugar and eggs to the butter and mix well. Add flour and cocoa and mix to make a smooth batter. Pour the batter into a greased 9-inch (22-cm) baking tin dusted with flour. Press the berries into the batter. Bake the cake for about half an hour. It should be sticky in the middle.

If your blackberries are frozen, let them thaw completely. Serve the cake with blackberries and whipped cream.

6–8 SERVINGS
5 ⅓ oz (150 g) butter
1 ¼ cups (250 g) sugar
2 eggs
⅔ cup (80 g) all-purpose flour
3–4 tbsp cocoa
butter and flour for the cake tin
⅔–¾ cup (100 g) blackberries, fresh or
    frozen

TO SERVE:
about 1 ½ cups (200 g) blackberries,
    fresh or frozen
whipped cream

Chocolate Mousse with Almond Sprinkles

It is nice to serve this mousse with almond sprinkles and some berries, or just berries if you don't have time to make the sprinkles.

Carefully melt the raw sugar in a heavy-bottomed pot. Add the almonds and stir with a wooden spoon to combine. Pour the mix into a heatproof container lined with parchment paper. Watch your fingers, because the melted sugar is really hot. Let it cool.

Break the chocolate into smaller pieces. Melt it in a bowl over a pot of steaming water. Remove from the heat and let the chocolate cool down to a warm temperature.

Whip the cream, but not too much. Add egg yolks and icing sugar to the chocolate, and mix well. Mix the chocolate mixture and the whipped cream until you have an even chocolate mousse. Pour it into individual bowls and let them sit in the fridge for 1–2 hours.

Chop the almonds with a large knife and sprinkle it over the mousse before serving.

8 SERVINGS
⅔ cup (127 g) raw sugar
½ cup (60 g) almonds
3 ½ oz (100 g) dark chocolate, 70%
    cacao
1 ¼ cups (300 ml) whipping cream
egg yolks
1–2 tbsp icing sugar

Packing Up

"Bye, Gotland; bye, house; bye, beaches, horses, little lambs . . ."

I'm in the backseat of dad's white Volkswagen camper. The window is rolled down, and I'm trying to soak up the last of the summer breeze. School starts tomorrow. Amelia, Amanda, and I are saying goodbye to everything beautiful here. I'm crying, as usual.

In our family we all suffer from pretty severe separation anxiety. We hate it when we're forced to leave the people we love and the places we adore. Closing the door on summer and leaving the country home is a strange feeling for all of us. I can tell when it is time. The wind brings an air of fall, the sun shines less bright, and the silence is different. We all have our own way of ending the summer. Amanda just picks up and leaves, leaving the summer behind. I think it's because she doesn't want to see the change. She never takes things with her, so that in her memory the country home can stay the same, and the summer there is eternal. I'm exactly the opposite. I clean and pack as if I am never coming back. I write goodbye letters in the guestbook, and put everything in its place. The house is my time machine. All past summers are saved here. I am preserving summer here, sealing it so that I'm ready to start anew. And it's as if next summer might arrive faster this way.

No summer is alike. We might be in the same place, with the same people, but every summer is different, with a different mood and different food. We find a new favorite spot in the garden, rearrange furniture, and buy new things. Old floral cups and plates are put away to make room for new floral flea market finds. The one thing that is constant is our love for this place.

Yet another magical summer has passed. The car is loaded, and tomorrow we're switching nature for asphalt and cement. We say goodbye like we always do: "Bye, house . . . We'll be back soon!"

—Hannah

Leftover Pie

Set your oven to 400° F (200° C).

Work together all the ingredients for the dough, and press it into a pie tin. Bake for about 10 minutes. Remove from the oven and raise the temperature to 450° F (225° C).

Mix eggs with milk or cream, or a milk and cream mixture. Add salt and pepper. Chop raw chicken or bacon, if using. Add vegetables, cheese, and any meat to the pie crust, and pour the egg mixture over everything. Top with grated hard cheese. Cook in the oven for about half an hour, or until the egg mixture is firm.

It is nice to serve this pie with a salad. Take whatever you have and make a vinaigrette with olive oil, vinegar, Italian salad seasoning, and herb salt.

CRUST:
1 ½ cups (185 g) all-purpose flour
½ cup (125 g) butter
2 tbsp water

FILLING:
4 eggs
1 ¾ cups (40 ml) milk, cream, or both, whatever is left in the fridge
other leftovers, such as broccoli, onion, bacon, feta cheese...
leftover hard cheese

Barbecue Hash with Yogurt Sauce

Dice the meat. Because it's already cooked, add it to the hash toward the end. Chop the vegetables and halloumi into equally sized chunks. Keep the cherry tomatoes whole.

Sauté the onion, vegetables, and halloumi in olive oil. Add the tomatoes toward the end. When the vegetables are al dente, add the meat and a splash of veal stock, or beef bouillon.

Toast the nuts in a little bit of olive oil in a different pan. Top the hash with the nuts when it's done. Serve with yogurt sauce.

Yogurt sauce: Pour yogurt or crème fraîche into a bowl, and add chopped herbs. Season to taste with herb salt and salad seasoning.

ingredients that are often leftover in the fridge:
scraps of meat from last night's barbecue
onions
asparagus or other vegetables
halloumi
cherry tomatoes
olive oil
veal stock, or beef bouillon
nuts

YOGURT SAUCE:
yogurt or crème fraîche
any fresh herbs you have on hand, such as mint or basil
Herbamare herb salt
Italian salad seasoning

Meringue Sundae

Layer ice cream, whipped cream, berries, fruit, and meringue on a large serving platter. Drizzle generously with caramel sauce.

If you have a meringue cake base: Place the meringue on the platter and layer ice cream, whipped cream, berries, and fruit on it. Drizzle with caramel sauce.

all the ice cream in your freezer
whipped cream
all the fruit and berries you have left
meringues or meringue cake base
caramel sauce

Yummy Caramel Sauce

Mix all the ingredients in a heavy-bottomed pot. Cook until the sauce thickens to a good consistency. Stir the sauce with a wooden spoon a few times. The longer you let it cook, the thicker the sauce will become.

Let the sauce cool before pouring it over the sundae.

¾ cup (200 ml) whipping cream
¾ cup (200 ml) golden syrup, or corn syrup
¾ cup (170 g) sugar
2 tbsp cocoa
1 tsp vanilla extract

Index

Design: Pernilla Blomqvist
Cover photo: Amelia Widell
Photos: Amelia Widell
Prepress: Elanders Fälth& Hässler, Värnamo

Skyhorse Publishing books may be purchased in bulk at special
discounts for sales promotion, corporate gifts, fund-raising, or
educational purposes. Special editions can also be created to
specifications. For details, contact the Special Sales Department,
Skyhorse Publishing, 307 West 36th Street, 11th Floor, New York,
NY 10018 or info@skyhorsepublishing.com.

Skyhorse® and Skyhorse Publishing® are registered trademarks of
Skyhorse Publishing, Inc.®, a Delaware corporation.

www.skyhorsepublishing.com

10 9 8 7 6 5 4 3 2 1

Library of Congress Cataloging-in-Publication Data is available on
file.

Print ISBN: 978-1-62914-660-7
Ebook ISBN: 978-1-63450-111-8

Cover design by Eric Kang

Printed in China